A Sea of Emotion

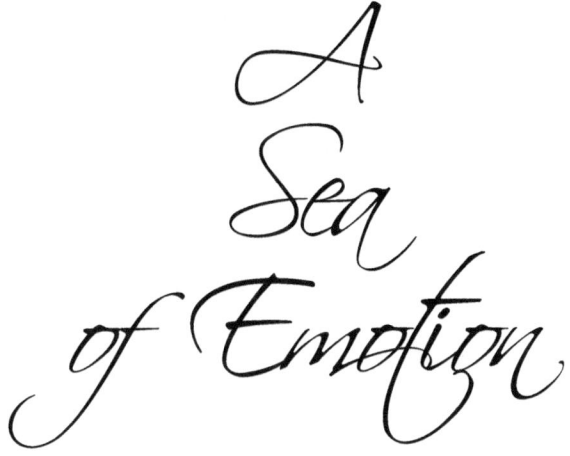

A Sea of Emotion

KERRY L. MARZOCK

ReadersMagnet, LLC

DEDICATION

The emotions within this book can be attributed to Richard, who I have loved dearly, and who has faithfully stood beside me for thirty years, never failing to love me. And to Sela, who opened my heart and proved that love is far too precious to let slip away. To my parents and brother, who have always loved and believed in me, even when I pushed the envelope and made life very interesting. I love you all so very much.

ACKNOWLEDGEMENT

To Ron Kisner who provided me the opportunity to realize a life-long dream of mine. To all my wonderful friends who have read my work, believing in me and any talent I might have. To Karol Choate, who became more than just a friend to me so very long ago when I so desperately needed someone to confide to in what seems a completely different lifetime. You will always be very special to me.

A Sea of Emotion
Copyright © 2022 by Kerry Marzock

Published in the United States of America
ISBN   Paperback: 978-1-957312-85-9
ISBN   eBook: 978-1-957312-86-6

All rights reserved. No part of this publication may be reproduced, stored in a retrieval system or transmitted in any way by any means, electronic, mechanical, photocopy, recording or otherwise without the prior permission of the author except as provided by USA copyright law.

The opinions expressed by the author are not necessarily those of ReadersMagnet, LLC.

ReadersMagnet, LLC
10620 Treena Street, Suite 230 | San Diego, California, 92131 USA
1.619. 354. 2643 | www.readersmagnet.com

Book design copyright © 2022 by ReadersMagnet, LLC. All rights reserved.

Cover design by Kent Gabutin
Interior design by Dorothy Lee

TABLE OF CONTENTS

A Sea Of Emotion 13
Breakable Heart 14
Heart Made Of Glass 15
The Price Of Love 16
Children In The Darkness 17
Someday My Love Will Come 20
Darkness Falling 21
Life Of Shadows 22
Dance Of Hearts 23
Window Of Teardrops 24
Love And Pain 26
When The Dream Ends 27
Upon The Breath Of Morning 28
The Dawn Has Come And Gone 29
Enwrapped Within Your Arms 31
Shadows In The Moonlight 32
An Ocean Of Chaos 33
Tattered Valentine 35
I See You In Shadows 36
The Scarecrow Waltz 37
Whispers Of Love 39
Fog Of Lonely Hearts 41
Winter Winds 42
Weapons Of Bitterness 43
Sacred Vows 44
Crying In The Darkness 46

Piano Nights 48

The Unforgiving Sky 50

Broken Love 51

Bitter Sweet Surrender 52

Saying Good-Bye To Memories 53

For Just One Moment 54

Desperation 55

Romance In The Rain 57

Always A Kiss 58

Sounds Of Dying Love 59

Beside You In The Morning 60

Christmas Morning With Love 62

Fires Of Love 64

Sail Away 66

Sometimes Dreams 67

Don't Come True 67

This Hold You Have On Me 69

When I....My Love 70

Devil's At My Doorstep 71

Forgotten 73

Dream Of Roses 76

Can Love Be Trusted? 78

On The Far Side Of Tranquility 80

Sands Of Innocence 83

Tree Of Loneliness 85

Bitter Words 86

The Lady From Yesterday 87

When Blackbirds Fly 89

The Lonely Shroud.. 90
In The Darkness.. 91
Panic 93
Creature #1 96
Creature #2 97
Creature#3 99
Blood On The Moon 100
A Lonely Poet... 101
You Take My Breath Away~ ~ 102
Bridge Of Discovery... 103
What If Today.. 105

A SEA OF EMOTION

I feel like I'm bobbing out of control, aimlessly adrift,
on a starkly desolate and ever so lonely sea,
lying within a tiny lifeboat overflowing with tears.
Seems I'm drowning in a sea of emotion meant only for me.

Far ahead is an island where true love awaits.
A special someone who I treasure, that I so adore.
However, behind is a person who loves me, I know that.
Part of a life l can't deal with much more.

I seem to be trapped in a maze of despair.
Tears won't stop flowing, hope's fading away.
I stare at the future, living with those who don't care,
that the true love awaiting could disappear if l stay.

So I float ever alone on this cruel sea of emotion,
all hopes and dreams of true love fading.
Seems I'm a prisoner of fate, it binds me so tight.
God I can't breathe; I can feel my heart breaking.

But for those who don't care how I feel deep inside,
don't worry or fret, I could lose my salvation.
The guilt you have offered is the shackles that tie me,
to float ever lost and afraid on this sea of emotion.

BREAKABLE HEART

The heart is your existence, your purpose,
your strength. It is your death, your
downfall, your weakness.
It is soft and pliable like cool, moist clay,
able to be molded in the hands of a lover.
It is hard like cold, gray steel, unable to
be scaled when securely locked and tightly sealed.
It grins in the heat of the sun, and flows
serenely under the comfort of moonbeams.
It laughs in the bright sunlight and quietly
sobs amid the peaceful curtain of rainfall.
It has the smoothness of old, worn leather, and
the sheerness of pure silk, and yet can feel
the icy clutch of winter's grip, or hear the soft
whispering cascade of leaves falling to the ground.
The heart is your existence, your purpose,
your strength. It is your death, your
downfall, your weakness.
Gossamer in its thickness, pristine in its
pureness, it is but forever the breakable heart.

HEART MADE OF GLASS

Shining crystal clear, pristine within early daylight,
softly shimmering underneath a watchful moon
of mighty Aphrodite, the heart of glass is
warmed by the golden, midday sun, or
chilled by a frosty, midnight breeze.

It quietly sobs at the merest trembling of lost love and
softly shatters under somber thoughts of nevermore.
Falling inside a bottomless window of emotion, it
reflects the vibrant colors of evening primrose
from the smiling eyes of impulsive Eros.

Yet within the early sighs of mornings' light, or sleeping
softly under the lacy touch of smiling midnight, the
heart of glass has the power to survive a jagged
teardrop, or the crushing weight of loves'
departure in the dreariness of twilight.

As a mirrored reflection of life's remembered past,
I gaze with fondness at memories saved within a
pristine heart made of glass!

THE PRICE OF LOVE

The magic of love is innocent and oh so gentle,
rising and falling within the pureness of emotion.
A soft touch of fingertips, a whispering caress of lips,
or a breathless kiss of sweet adulation!
Reaching desperately with anxious fingers
for an embrace which the price of love allows!
People may change, or often grow apart,
with miles of years in between, while searching for
answers that are not there, an old love fading away.
Knowing full well that something wondrous will die
if your choice is but to stay!
The price of love is a heart screaming out of control,
a mind floundering at sea!
Staring with guilt at possibly a life destroyed,
only to scrape and claw for happiness through a trail
of yesterday's scattered debris!
Tears flowing freely from a lifetime of spurned memories,
feeling the only way to secure true love
is to watch an old one die!
Totally aware that the painful price of love
will forever remain alive!

KERRY MARZOCK

CHILDREN IN THE DARKNESS

Can you hear their cries?
*
*
*

Their shallow, frightened voices echo off our minds
as tearful pleas of help go unanswered,
lost children whose happiness we cannot find.
They lie torn and broken on tiny beds
within empty rooms of soulless houses,
while real life creatures that they've come to dread
hover in the darkness, preying on their fears,
greedily consuming such tragic tears.
It is an evil menace that devours innocence.
A vile thief of dreams devoid of all humanity,
an ominous beast that hides its fangs and claws
behind vacant smiles and enticing candy.

But do we listen?
Can we hear them calling?

They ARE our children and yet our ears are closed.
When they speak we do not believe them.
When we have the chance to expose
and prosecute, our courts and juries succumb
to the glitz of glamour and fame,
crumble under laws to protect the accused once again.
Yet a monster is a monster, no matter how

poor or destitute, no matter how
rich or famous.

Not only do our children fear the beast,
but become the manipulative pawns
of those who would dig for gold.
Who would thus be spurned and tumble away
from their parent's love which has
turned bitter and cold.
*
*

Listen closely....... can you hear their tortured screams?
Do you feel the loneliness and
degradation,
the guilt, the shame, the pain?
*
*

Stop for a second and just listen
*
*
*
*
*

It is not the laughter of innocent dreams,
but rather the terror from distressing nightmares.
It is the anguished sound of a child crying,
the snicker of the beast leering at us.
It is the deadly silence of our courts echoing in our hearts.
With each passing chance to heed their frightened cries
'we allow one more child to lie broken,
a sweet little girl with soft curls to lie dying,

yet another small, brave boy with a handsome smile
to cower cringing in the darkness.... crying,
so afraid to speak out,
his strangled words of terror and abandonment
left unspoken.

*

*

*

Just listen
For somewhere a monster is grinning.
Sadly, within shadows another child is sobbing.
Tragically, a young, forlorn boy or a terrified little girl
realizes there is not a chance of being
saved, that to speak out means
there is no one there to
hear them.

*

*

*

Listen to the silence~ for it is the disappearance
of our children's innocence
slowly dying in the
darkness.

SOMEDAY MY LOVE WILL COME

Your smile shimmers before me.
Reach out~~ grasping, touching, hoping.
Fingers anxiously spreading tears atop a desolate sea,
heart still desperately coping.... for~
more of your tranquil, blue eyes.
Searching distant shores,
echoes of your voice
lying upon silent
and lonesome
sighs.

Your warm embrace still so real
and yet so very far away,
thoughts of how
it used to be, should be, supposed to be.
My haunted dreams quietly hearing you say,
"Honey, I will love you forever," but
does forever really mean never?
Desires spread before us on fields
of distant heather, afloat on
fractured hopes
that someday love will come
to hold my heart again.
That true devotion
is never said
and done.

DARKNESS FALLING

I feel the breath of darkness bleeding
into the final, sagging rays of daylight,
with urgent thoughts of you now pleading
in silent supplication upon the night.

Let me cleanse myself with moonbeams
to wash away these nagging sorrows,
my life afloat on distant dreams
that scatter hopes of bright tomorrows.

At times, this haunting pain is so intense
I can hear the song of wayward heartbeats
continue calling out for such sweet providence,
a wish my touch still lay upon your cheek.

On whispered sighs the pouting moon stares
down from dark and lonely skies,
our hopes and dreams gone far too soon
with barely a taste of paradise.

I gently close my eyes to hear your voice
softly say, "I love you," into my ear,
but then "It's time to go," was not my choice
as darkness fell upon these lonely tears.

LIFE OF SHADOWS

I've walked this earth in shadows
gently veiled in timeless shades of gray,
mixed with frantic tears of long tomorrows,
softly fading atop whispered breath of yesterday.
~*~*~*~*~
There were moments in my life,
dark and brooding times of confusion
when attempts to adumbrate cries of strife
sang alone ~ barely existing within optical illusion.
~*~*~*~
Dust of stars enshroud my dreams
which dance in shadows, a black and gray
conundrum of sharply lancinating moonbeams,
starry teardrops kissing a darkly shaded doorway.
Cerulean thoughts, upon neon bright tomorrows,
so long at sea in anguished moonlight.
This life of somber shadows
masquerading inside
madly flickering
candlelight.
~*~*~
~*~*~
~*~
~
*

DANCE OF HEARTS

Thy love rests on the breath of early morn,
soft hair spread askew across a pillowed sea
as we commit once more our love thus sworn,
lips bathed in warm sunshine when I kiss thee.
O romance doth descend a top our hearts,
whence to brush sweet memories of last night
across my mind, thy wish to never part
from your arms that embraced this love so tight.
Soft whisperings of your gentle fingers
caressed my skin with erotic foreplay~~~
sighing, eyes transfixed, as passion lingers.
I entreat this dream to forever stay.
Please take mine hand before this love departs
while we swirl as one to our dance of hearts.

WINDOW OF TEARDROPS

Staring through this stark window of teardrops
my thoughts desperately search for you.
The miles between us just seem
to grow farther and farther apart,
blowing trees whispering your name.
A tear trickles down
the dark, barren pane of glass,
solitary and so
alone~~~

Clutching a warm cup of coffee between my hands,
I'm softly reminded of just how nice it was
to snuggle closely up beside you,
searching for those little spots that brought pleasure
and a contented smile to your face.
I wonder if I will ever again explore
those sweet valleys of Paradise, fields of roses
and caverns of desire.
I wonder~~~

KERRY MARZOCK

So much against us from the very beginning,
it seems like we were never meant to be.
To have met at a different time, a different place,
within another dream would've been heaven.
I think fate tries to be the big equalizer,
but like any of the obstacles we've already conquered,
this one can be overcome as well.
Do you want it as badly as I?
Do....You dream of us together?
I swipe a hand across my eyes,
windows to your heart,
these teardrops now
my own~~~

LOVE AND PAIN

Love
and pain
together
spell disaster.
Love with jealousy
breeds contempt and deceit.
Love so simple becomes hard
like layers of volcanic rock.
Animosity begets hatred
that simmers from boiling to eruption.
A song of romance once sung with passion
now grates upon the ears and blinds all
possible ways of forgiveness.
Tears have become your escape,
the end of love's sad song.
But in the death of
pain and anger,
a dream of
love is
yours.

WHEN THE DREAM ENDS

I hate to close my eyes.
It's when darkness comes upon me now.
Darkness so painfully thick
there's no damn breath left to take.
Breath that once belonged to you,
now stolen from me,
stolen on dreams made of tears.
Dreams that used to flourish under a
sky of smiles, of hopes, of...of...
nothing now,
just this blackness.
Your sweet smile no longer
held within my trembling hands,
trembling that used to come
from your velvet touch.
A touch I never thought I would feel...
never thought you'd stop
saying
I love you
But you have and I don't
know why...why?
Maybe I'll just never know.
Maybe I'll never love again, maybe...
just why
the dream finally ended.
Maybe…

A SEA OF EMOTION

UPON THE BREATH OF MORNING

I can feel your quiet heartbeat
even before the peace of morning
gently shakes my needs awake.
A soft summer breeze
jostles my silent urging,
your love now mine to take.

Gossamer sunlight like Chinese silk
flows dreamily across my thighs,
reawakening our passion of last night.
Your touch as soft as buttermilk,
my skin once more alive
to sweet desires you now invite.

Let my eager hands roam to lands
I've explored so much before,
no fear of ever getting lost.
Let us once more lie on sands
of bliss, your ship alit upon my shore,
two hearts and souls now crossed.

"Hey, are you awake?"
as I slide softly into your embrace,
hearts racing, lips uniting, sheer Paradise.
It's so nice to welcome daybreak
with our smiles upon your pillowcase,
breath of morning to entice.

THE DAWN HAS COME AND GONE

When icy, brittle winds of winter have
angrily shaved the leaves from late November,
I hear the loons sing their haunting song
of misty woebegone, our smiles
now come and gone ~

I can still see your eyes through shades of fog
in those quiet moments just before
desire spreads apart the dawn.
Salty tears mingle with cool showers of
April days, then springs to touch mayflowers and
caress the orange of robin redbreast, words of
passion thus expressed, sweet lips
once felt, now gone ~

Your lush and hungry kisses once more
my early morning treasure, forever
gentle as the waking sun.

Small pearls of summer perspiration trickle
down a path once traced upon my spine, silky fingers
always gentle, so heavenly divine, your eyes my
heart's reflection as fall lingers, a love
we tasted, but sadly gone ~

A SEA OF EMOTION

I feel your arms embrace me as I desperately
fight to ward off one more lonely
disenchanted morn.

Fragile snowflakes quietly sift down from steel-gray
skies, memories of you dancing within velvet moonlight.
I close my eyes, a year of tears guiding our way,
Imploring you to stay, but knowing your
heart has come and gone ~

I so hate the hours between midnight and morning
because it means your love has whispered
good-bye and yet another dawn
has come and gone
~~forever~~

ENWRAPPED WITHIN YOUR ARMS

I close my eyes in silent rapture
as I feel the caress of your fingertips
trace a path upon the river of my desire,
~slowly~ down my pulsing neck to the curvature
of my breasts ~ a deep moan escaping my lips.
Oh sweet Lord, you have my mind afire.

Being held in your tight embrace
is like floating on a cloud of angel's wings.
I whisper in your ear, "Tell me that you love me,"
as I open my eyes to see the smiling look upon your face.
I yearn to have your tender touch play my heartstrings
in a symphony of love I thought would never be.

Your fingers move slowly down that river
of passion towards our verdant Garden of Paradise.
I can feel your push and then hear my excited purring,
letting my body arch up against your limbs all aquiver.
An exploding shower of lights rain down like fire and ice
and surround our thoughts of romance forever stirring.

I feel your sweet breath enclose my urgent lips
to take me sailing around the world on a sea of rainbows.
"I do love you so much," as your words caress my ears,
now afloat on this ocean of sheets, two lonely ships
docking in rhapsody under silky moon glow,
prisoners of love inside sensual tears.

SHADOWS IN THE MOONLIGHT

Silky whispers of moonlight
flowed softly through the open window,
painting silent shadows on my haunted mind.
A very lonely owl calls out your name as
I open my eyes for I had to know~~
was this but a dream, or were
you really here this time?

~~Gasping~~

I see your silhouette,
so erect and demanding that I come
to you, exploring your richest treasures.
I caress your shadow and feel desire
wrap itself around my muscles,
ecstasy on fire, grasping~~

~~Squeeze~~

my heart bursting, swollen
from passion not felt in far too long.
Our lips in such sweet surrender,
friction of our skin blazing
in hot, burning embers,

~~~~~Deeper~~~~~
Gone…

KERRY MARZOCK

AN OCEAN OF CHAOS

Alone ~ I lie frail, untouched
nearly unconscious,

watching love float
across an ocean of chaos.
Our future unknown,
time standing still,
worried your desire for me

has dried up.
Do you miss my soft laugh,
the silkiness of my touch,
the gentle press of my scarlet lips on yours?
I lie unmoving,

caring not what happens now,
hot sun no longer shining.
Cold~~~
So damn cold here.
I miss the delicious motion of you,

pressed firmly against me,
two minds as one.
My fingers clutched to your soft pillow
leaving prints that have
no meaning now.

A SEA OF EMOTION

I reach out to touch your essence
left behind as my desire rises,
but no movement.
Now just a person alone,
worried that life without you

has no meaning,
no future.
Will you ever come back to me?
My hopes still so high for
I will always love you!

TATTERED VALENTINE

She sat so quietly at the kitchen table,
this woman of dreams now lost in thoughts.
Her steeping tea with the nutty aroma of hazel,
filling the dimly lit room with memories of whatnots.
In her nervous hands she held a card,
lightly yellowed, slightly worn, corner torn.
A tear fell softly upon her cheek for the loving bard
whose words she read aloud, his devoted love thus sworn.
"Oh my dearest, sweetest Celeste, I miss you so!
These days feel cold, my nights are long, the skies so dark!
You are the star that guides my way in warmth of moon glow!
You are the woman of my dreams to whom I gave my heart!"
Tears now flowed freely as she thought of her beloved Sam,
so tall and handsome, blue eyes glowing with his love.
She was aware of what he had shed for peace in Vietnam,
more than just blood under dark clouds of war above.
She held this tattered card of hearts to her breast
as she heard the hint of movement from behind.
"Good morning my lovely, sweetest Celeste.
I love you! Will you be my Valentine?"
She stood and hugged this man
like she had done for years.
"Oh, I love you too Sam, "
in love's sweet tears!
"You'll forever be
my sweetest
Valentine!"

A SEA OF EMOTION

I SEE YOU IN SHADOWS

I close my eyes to the whispers of night
and all I can see are varied shades of you and me,
sitting together across an ocean of sweet candlelight,
a flickering soft flame dancing on a gentle breeze.
Then I slowly open my eyes to know
only deepening gray shadows.

Strolling down a grocery aisle,
rubbing shoulders and touching fingertips,
basking in the blush of your warm and loving smile.
I close my eyes and can taste your sweet lips.
But when I open them I see the glow
has faded to dark blue shadows.

Shadows that quietly slither in and out
of my conscious reality that you may never be here,
amid these cheerless walls of murkiness and self-doubt.
The haunting wind-blown sound my silent tears
now play as they're struck in rapid arpeggio
on piano keys within charcoal shadows.

This day has come to a lonely end now,
sliding beneath cool sheets that whisper your name.
I reach out for you with anxious fingertips and wonder how
a love that felt so right, so natural, could feel the pain
of broken heartstrings atop the fading moon glow,
fallen now upon dismal midnight shadows.

THE SCARECROW WALTZ

An enraptured moon of pumpkin-harvest orange,
gently caressed the fields with a soothing lunar flow,
early winter now picked clean by sleeping farmers
and a flock of overly fat, but sassy crows.

Upon the stroke of midnight, lonely clouds shall dance
while a glittering chorus of stars sing in perfect harmonies.
It's time for anxious lovers to cast a wistful glance
and let their deep desires sail upon romantic seas.

He hung forlornly upon a cross of wooden sticks,
this man of yellow straw and tattered clothes.
Waiting patiently all year, he stared through eyes transfixed
at a lonely figure clad in a torn dress of faded primrose.

She stared with urgent longing at this man within her dreams,
a long and lonely year gone by without feeling his tender touch.
The tingling rush of fingertips like soft and velvet moonbeams,
or the whispering caress of lips she sorely missed so much.

At midnight, stardust rained down from an amber-painted sky,
glowing brightly in a breathtaking display of sparkling tears.
Two rekindled heartbeats sharing a note of grateful sighs,
their eyes alive to dance on yet another New Year's~~~Eve.

A SEA OF EMOTION

Frayed shirt, ragged pants and straw hat now replaced
with a tuxedo of brilliant black and satin lapels.
Moving quickly across the field he held her slender waist,
to welcome her inviting lips to his, entranced within her spell.

Lush auburn hair cascaded softly down around her breasts,
the blue silk of her gown whispering a quiet ~~~ "I love you."
Dancing to the waltz of scarecrows, he held her to his chest
within a tight embrace, praying this night would but continue.

Just one sweet waltz this evening was all they were allowed to dance.
With the music sadly fading, they slowly returned to their places.
But right before their eyes went shut, they cast a tearful glance
to see their loving smiles still etched upon their faces.

WHISPERS OF LOVE

I gently close my eyes and crave
the tender push of yours lips to mine,
a kiss that may cause the angels to weep.
Such subtle pressures of arousal
that build in warm waves from the inner core
of my sweet desire for you.
Probing and exploring to greater depths
than even I thought I could never hope to find.

A sweet taste of spearmint as your breath
whispers softly like exotic silk
brushing my tingling skin.

"My God...."

I'm on fire as your knee
whispers teasingly against the creamy surface
of my trembling thighs.

A SEA OF EMOTION

"Open up for me...."

Your words caress my ears in a whispering sigh,
as I lie on a bed of pink orchids, lost
in a cloud of grateful tears.

"I love you...."Whispered on the tips of my breasts, my mind
now exploding in a living rainbow of light.

"Oh Lord, please...."

Let these whispers last all through this blessed night!

KERRY MARZOCK

FOG OF LONELY HEARTS

A thick, questioning fog,
dismal shade of sadly worn silver,
rolls across the landscape and into my heart.
The mournful howl of a lonely dog
lies harshly upon my ears as I stare bewildered
at dreams of being together, now forever split apart.

Heads of spidery trees
forlornly extend their skeletal limbs
like desolate scarecrows pleading supplication.
I realized there were no guarantees!
Lost within gray shadows, wondering how to begin
life without you, love now turned to silent desperation.

A sobbing raven circles overhead,
landing abruptly on the edges of a prayer,
pecking insanely at the blue windows of my soul.
So many things left unsaid!
Feeling I've been deserted and left behind
while my lost emotions spin further out of control.

Snowy gray seagulls slice
through the mist like ghostly apparitions,
searching for pieces of my frail and shattered dreams.
All thoughts of sweet paradise
carried off upon their mocking suppositions.
This fog of lonely hearts alive with haunting screams!

WINTER WINDS

Snowflakes fall softly from charcoal painted skies
like the tears of angels as heaven sighs.
They rest quietly upon frozen ground
that now shivers from nights of cruel sorrows.
Amid naked trees whose summer attire
has long since been blown away,
a steady wintry wind dances slowly around
weakening sunlight of the fading day,
forever frowning at thoughts of bleaker tomorrows.

The tears of lonely lovers
echo painfully against the smiling winds,
as if they see and hear the breaking of your heart.
Like the ghostly moaning of lost love
the empty treetops sway angrily from side to side,
the haunting song of broken dreams
hanging from beseeching tips of empty limbs.
Behind those tired walls of sadness,
the biting winter wind spins and screams
while lost hearts are eternally buried
as ravens fly and angels cry.

WEAPONS OF BITTERNESS

Like a sharp edged knife, it slices through happiness,
all the painful layers of frustrated emotions flayed open.
Hands securely tied to a post, the whip bearing witness.
Stinging tears heralding an ending that had to happen.

Venomous words as deadly and dangerous as any bullet,
accurately fired from a gun made of animosity and anger.
Insults and inflammatory names exploding from its' mouth,
creating wounds inflicted by someone who was now a stranger.

A fierce arrow tainted with poison from years of neglect.
Injured from being taken for granted, expected to provide,
the heavy weight of responsibility destroying all respect.
Knowing you sacrificed for years, that you absolutely tried.

With alcohol abuse erasing any luster from love that used to be.
Taking the gleam of happiness and painting it sadly dreary.
Now thoughts of worry creating heavy pages of angry deceit,
while realizing that my pangs of guilt are far, far too heavy.

When love erodes and friendship fades you know it's dying.
They were the glue and cement keeping a relationship alive.
No more hugs, or kisses, or "I love you!" with any meaning.
Now fully aware, without any doubt, that I will survive!

SACRED VOWS
Dedicated to John & Hillary
(10/30/04)

He took one look at her exquisite features
~~ and he knew~~
his heart was hers for eternity.
She glanced at his handsome, rugged face
~~and she knew~~
her love was his from now and to infinity.

They warmly held each other's quivering hands,
though shaking not from fright.
It was more from the jangle of nerves
for they were about to carry each other
to new, uncharted lands
where their loving embrace would expand the night.

He fell into the deep, hypnotic pools of her eyes
~~ and softly whispered~~
"I'll love you forever and vow to you right now
that our life together I will always treasure."

She smiled, her heartbeat joining his as one,
~~and whispered back~
"I'll love you too, and pledge my love
and my life to forever be your wife."

The glow now surrounding them was not just
from the golden rings they wore on their fingers,
or from their love now supremely blessed
in heaven's good grace.
It was more the warmth and tenderness of
love's serenity from God's smiling face.

Their unity thus pledged
with hearts forever joined as one now,
they tightly held hands and strolled down the
aisle of marriage to spend the rest
of their lives together,
~forever~

CRYING IN THE DARKNESS

The somber roar of silence deafening,
thick, oppressive darkness all but smothering.
I sit alone in a quiet house, yet not really alone.
The soothing stillness of night sliced apart
with painful, broken, hollow breathing.
Words of misunderstanding slamming a conflicted heart
that now feels icy cold, turned to solitary stone.

Suddenly the crashing of a teardrop on a cheek,
doing its' best to crack the frigid stillness.
Running like a burning river down skin
already reddened from confusion and stress.
Tracing a journey of loneliness and sorrow,
while trying to maneuver through a battlefield
in a war to repel what others expect of you tomorrow.

The wailing of a clock counting off the confusing years,
chanting, "Who am I?" "What am I?" "Why me?"
Identity forsaken in a world where "norms" of society
are painfully unrelenting, unforgiving, replete with fears.
Knowing with passion who you are and need to be.
Desperately trying to save what's left of sanity.
Sadly, for some, ending tragically!

Yet the loneliness of night surrenders to revealing daylight,
fingertips of darkness disappearing with the moonlight.
Identity still confused with an inner voice sobbing,
dreaming so desperately to make life better.
Reaching deep inside to warmly embrace another.
while giving strength to dreams far too long suppressed.

Discovering grateful answers to questions long repressed.
No more hiding in the shadows, or crying in the night,
knowing who you are with meaning and conviction.
Uncaring what others think due to their own repression.

It's your life, your own desperate plight,
while you travel down a path of constant transition.
No longer crying in the darkness,
forever smiling in the light.

PIANO NIGHTS

Sometimes when I lie alone,
eyes tightly closed
I can hear the piano keys of my life ~

ivory white
in their brilliance…

solemnly black
under subdued silence…

tastefully melodic
within such sweet perfection…

angrily raging
over misconstrued abstraction…

and yet~
sadly, out of tune,
missing a beat here and there,
nervous fingertips running up and down
lonesome arpeggios,
teardrops reaching to who knows where.

Flats of purple haze,
sharps of graying days,
softly singing moonbeams sigh
to the melody of
unrequited good-byes~

the fading blues
of love's unfinished symphony
dies out in my haunted eyes ~

but when I cry,
I cry for only you.

A SEA OF EMOTION

THE UNFORGIVING SKY

As a child I lifted up innocent eyes, forever scratching the sky,
only to feel searing shafts of light slice easily through my pain,
piercing for a moment the blanket of confusion and dismay,
a mind locked in battle over thoughts I was powerless to explain.

Closing troubled eyes, I would scramble up those rays of escape,
searching desperately for answers, forever asking "Why?"
Wishing I could be born anew, thoughts and physical desires
trying so desperately to merge, abandoning a world full of lies.

At night I would kneel and pray, watching stars twinkle high above,
blinking at me with full understanding, consoling and soothing.
The tender moon, especially when full, smiled with eyes of love,
telling me, "It'll be okay!" as I lie frightened and alone, crying.

Sweet infinite night, you held no answers then, vast and bottomless.
Oh, twinkle, twinkle little star, please answer, who am I?
Mirror, mirror on the wall, whose reflection do I see? Not me!
Tears converged, my dreams again unfulfilled by an unforgiving sky.

That was then, young and alone, desperate to find a meaning.
I knew that God would not forsake me, there had to be a way.
Sparkling stars were winks of understanding, not unforgiving.
My tears craved understanding, while the mirror held the truth.

BROKEN LOVE

Love is so brittle, like the tiniest, frailest twig
from a massive and mighty tree of oak.
One minute seeming unbreakable,
while in the next feeling ever lost and alone,
shaken and broke.

Binding chains of love, at times so strong,
fastened securely to stars in the heavens above.
My tears of sadness falling freely
as romance turns wrong, trying to comprehend
the passage of unfulfilled love.

Remembering so many sweet kisses,
warm and tender embraces, now all but
memories, lying forlorn and crying.
Feeling the pain of loss, while searching for traces
of reasons why, all hopes and dreams dashed and dying.

There was a time when our loving smiles lit up the sky,
never having remorseless thoughts of sadness,
tender words of sincerity softly spoken.
Now sobs drifting aimlessly in one long, whispered sigh,
like branches of a dying oak, love now twisted and broken.

BITTER SWEET SURRENDER

Love is like a vicious battle
that just never seems to end.
Angry words that cause our hearts to
rattle with wounds so raw and painful
that they never seem to mend.

Sometimes I feel that living free
is the only way for me to go.
My body aching like limbs from a tree
inside a crying wind being bent and bowed
under the wailing moan of a lonely banshee.

I've heard that all is fair in love and war,
yet the scars I feel run true and deep.
All thoughts of sleep lost amid dreams of nevermore,
rusty and confused within an angry river of tears,
the only sound of battle is to hear me weep.

Oh surrender, sweet surrender,
I miss that smile, the twinkle in your eye,
our warm embrace, your touch so tender.
But the angry words were the weapons that I feared
broken memories all that's left as I watch love die.

SAYING GOOD-BYE TO MEMORIES

Memories scratched forlornly at the window panes,
their long and lonely tears streaking the trembling glass.
I could see the pleading look in their sorrowful eyes,
as I drove slowly away from a long and distant past.
"PLEASE don't go," they called to me, **"we'll be so all alone!"**

I tried to remember back amongst all the good times,
so long ago now that they seemed many miles away.
Sweet and smiling memories covered by insipid vibes, with
years of exploring love replaced by acts in a tragic play.
"PLEASE **stay,"** they pleaded, **"we love you so!"**

But some memories are like changing clouds in the sky,
massive and pristinely white, fiercely proud and free.
Others are black and ominous, more dead than alive,
beckoning storms that can destroy a love that used to be.
"PLEASE **come back,"** they sobbed, **"for we will surely die!"**

But no matter how hard I tried, emotion had disappeared.
Love was old and rusty, worn away, hollow kisses all 1 know.
Newer memories calling me to a love I have long awaited.
"PLEASE **remember us,"** they sadly lamented, **"Or we'll
fade away behind a tear stained window!"**

**"GOOD-BYE sweet memories,
part of a love that you created!"**

FOR JUST ONE MOMENT

Sometimes that's all it takes.
One glance, one touch, one kiss.
For just one moment,
and you know!

Your heart has been captured
within the instant embrace of love.
It was just one moment,
and you knew!

The desire to be close again
to that intoxicating heat of passion.
Waiting for one more moment,
that's all you pray for!

Sleepless nights and aching days,
bewildered by the urgent yearning.
Crying for one more moment,
that's all you dream of!

Amazingly it was just
one glance, one touch, one kiss.
For just one more moment!

DESPERATION

Are you there?

It's so dark, drowning in all-consuming
blackness, more than forever normal.
The lonely trickle of sadness, hot like a
solitary river of teardrops,
with a bitter loneliness crying out abnormally!
Only the tick, tock of my weeping heart
scratching the pervasive stillness.
NO! WAIT! Don't go, please **stop!**

Are you here?

Painful desperation sadly lingers,
amid the sallow, brooding silence.
It's so damn quiet within this
icy, frigid room of reticence.
Hope reaching out blindly for your
sweet and comforting presence.
But it's so empty, eerily soundless,
frightened fingers brushing nevermore.

Where are you?

A confused mind searching madly, but
in vain, piercing the omnipresent
shadows for even the slightest reason.
Why did your love disappear?
Hollowness aching for your touch,
a soft caress of fingertips, the loss
of one last loving season.
Now just loneliness lost within desperation!

ROMANCE IN THE RAIN

I gently held your hand as raindrops fell about us.
Leaves of reds and yellows and oranges fanned
haphazardly about, like the intricate pattern
of a beautifully handmade country quilt.
Our fingers interlaced in the romance of lovers,
with thumbs tenderly conveying romantic thoughts.

Merely content in feeling the warmth and tenderness
from a lifetime we had lovingly built together.
Strolling down paths that are now like well-worn
trails to the most intimate part of our souls.
Seeming to know each other better than it seemed
we could ever truly know ourselves.

Raindrops growing larger now, our arms intertwined,
skin glistening brightly, smiles radiant as ever.
My heart beating madly for a love I deeply treasured.
Our eyes reflecting the image of each other's face
as lips came together, pulses beginning to race.
Skies opening up now, thunder rolling like a runaway train.

Our love reflecting all the obstacles we had weathered.
It was purely simple, romance in the rain.

ALWAYS A KISS

I hold you so near me,
now and forever afraid to let go.
My fingers clutching desperately,
not wanting to sink below
a love that I would dearly miss
if it weren't always for that kiss.

A kiss, such an enchanting kiss
of lips that taste like the soothing,
velvety caress of moon glow.
The warm sparkle in your eyes,
enough to melt the silent snow that
drifts serenely down around us in a
cascading cloud of heavens' bliss.

Just a kiss, always a sweet, tender kiss,
which binds our love together in rhyme.
The glitter of stars twinkling ever so bright,
like Cupid's love struck, romantic eyes
that watch over us each and every night,
allowing the dream within my
maudlin heart to bloom and come alive.

For it's always a kiss.
Just that one very special kiss,
enough to last a lifetime!

SOUNDS OF DYING LOVE

CRASH!
The sound of two injured hearts hitting head on,
a road map of disaster merging in one more collision.
Glass crunching, metal grinding, happiness lost,
all final vestiges of love escaping in a cloud of icy frost.

SLAM!!
The door to love being thrown shut violently,
angry words trying to escape in a roar of finality.
"It's your fault!" "I hate you!!"
"You're the one who's wrong!!!"
Venomous insults mixed with soulful tears in loves' sad song.

SMASH!!!
Two hearts being crushed under loves' denial,
tear-stained pain of seeing death of love in its' arrival.
Feeling bitterness on wasted moments that came and went,
with too many years of anger mourning a song of sad lament.

BANG! BANG!!BANG!!!
Echoes from a canon ending loves' sweet reign,
now being drenched in a storm of thunder, wind and rain.
Abandoned signs hung forlornly outside a splintered door.

Crying....
"Sorry, but love has gone. It's not here anymore!"

A SEA OF EMOTION
BESIDE YOU IN THE MORNING

Rolling over onto my left side,
soft waves from the bed allow me to drift ever
closer to you on currents of love.
My wondering lips form a smile.... cause
I just know if I open my eyes but a hair
I fear you might not be truly there.

The awakening, twilight covered window to the day caresses
me with the breeze of your early morning breathing.
My eyes still closed as I greedily drink from
the joy of your nearness to me.
Oh God, you're so thinkable, drinkable, sinkable.

Still afraid to crack my eyes open for fear
that you'll disappear, I ease my right
leg up against yours, brushing ever so lightly
so as not to awaken you,
daring now to slowly slide my knee between the warm,
creamy fold of your thighs.

Ah you moan .... moving ever so slightly.
My heart races because I know you're really there.
Anxious fingertips of an exploring hand now
touching, feeling, caressing your lovely shoulder,
warmly basking within my daylight blessing.
You roll sensually towards me,
your lips now so close to mine that....

I can feel your breath blanket me underneath
the silkiness of angelic purity.

My eyes open wide, sipping in the perfection
of your face, now free-falling deeply
into love's good grace.
You open those deep, expressive eyes,
blinking in the sweetness of serenity.
Your lips form into that cute smile I love so much.

"Hey, honey, I love you," I softly whisper.
"Mmmmm, I love you too Baby!"

CHRISTMAS MORNING WITH LOVE

A soft whisper of white
falls quietly against the morning light.
It tenderly caresses the window panes
with an elegance of grace.

The festive twinkle of reds and greens,
hanging on the fragrant tree so bright,
shimmers like tinsel of a lover's dream
brushed serenely upon your face.

A crackling fire casts its' heavenly glow
off the happiness in our eyes.
It's Christmas morning you know,
as the angels smile and sigh.

KERRY MARZOCK

I snuggle my check to the warmth of your chest,
an arm draped over my shoulder in a loving embrace.
The thrill of anticipation as your fingertips
lightly touch the excitement of my breast.

Leaning into you I slide my lips toward yours,
overwhelmed by the tingle of passion I always feel
every time we kiss, as we explore
each other like we have so many times before.

As I gaze deeply into your eyes
I'm so thankful for your desire of me.
Our lips apart slightly, I whisper softly,
"Merry Christmas sweetheart, I love you so."

FIRES OF LOVE

I suddenly awake amid smothering duress,
frantically gasping for breath, fingers madly
clawing their way into frightening darkness.

Eyes searching for what?
For the nearness of happiness, so fearful of sadness.
Smelling the smoke of a life left burning,
while feeling the promise of a new one rising.
Hearing whispers from the ashes of a last love sobbing.

But searching for whom?
For the love I've been long awaiting.
The crackling flames of a past life glaring,
like the twisted sneer of a wicked demon,
pointing an accusing finger dripping with venom.

Searching for reasons why!
Answers still smoldering while too late in appearing.
Yet from the inferno rises a sweet reason for living,
tender warmth of two hearts creating their own fires,
healing wisps of smoke curling up, so forgiving.

Searching for a new beginning!
Holding you tight, lips caressing, heat growing from desire.
No longer ablaze with lost and hopeless thoughts, while
high above a glowing sun casts light upon a burnt out path.
I can feel Phoenix rising from a pyre of burning embers.
Searching for romance I had long ago remembered.
Now finding love amid the charred remaining aftermath.

SAIL AWAY

Standing on a quivering shoreline,
I gaze with eyes of hope across the undulating
ocean of my life wondering now if....
there will ever be room within
your world for me!

My love for you so boundless,
now forever lost and forlorn with
romantic thoughts of what might have been....
fearful a love that once seemed so sincere,
could be sadly lost amid waves of tears!

Remembering the tenderness of our embrace,
a sweet brush of lips so warm,
sensitive caress of exploring fingertips....
praying that you decide to stay,
though so afraid your ship might sail away....

forever...

SOMETIMES DREAMS DON'T COME TRUE

Closing my eyes, I willingly surrender to the romance
of the night. A time when angels sing and allow
the dream to slide over me once more like the
sensuous feel of black satin.

Reaching out with anxious fingers
I lovingly caress the smoothness of your cheek, the
lush silkiness of your hair, the angelic softness of your skin and
listen closely for the delicate sound of your voice.

With excitement that electric touch lingers....
my prayers a quiet plea that I'm actually lying beside you
inside the tender folds of midnight and to the
stretching dawn of early morning light.

I have felt the bewildering reality of your nearness
to me, seen the bright twinkle in your eyes
when you were happy and held you
close when your heart cried.

I've held your hand within the comforting warmth of my
own and tasted the sweetness of our embrace.
Constant thoughts of you spin madly inside my head
as I lie back once more on a lonely pillowcase.

Now it seems this beautiful dream is all l can hold onto,
my emotions painted with a darker shade of blue.
At night I still pray for a piece of happiness, but
I fear that sometimes dreams don't always come true!

THIS HOLD YOU HAVE ON ME

What is this hold you have on me?

It's like a magical spell,
some mystical rope that binds my
heart to yours.

It's like I'm floating wildly, out of control
. towards a frightening destiny on some
dangerous rocky shore where my heart
could get shattered and torn apart,
sinking forever in a sullen and lonely sea.

I'm so afraid I know I should heed the warnings.
But I can't....
for if l try and break the ties
that bind us, you might not be here....

in the morning!

WHEN I....MY LOVE

When I so gently close my thirsty eyes within the
soft, enchanting folds of midnight....
you are there!

When I pray upon my thoughts of hungry yearning,
nestled quietly on top of wishful stars....
you are on them!

When I feel deep desires seeking to caress warm lips,
letting fingertips explore a touch of heaven....
you are in them!

When I'm safely secure within my dreams of romance,
praying for just one more loving season....
you are the reason!

When I struggle lost and forlorn amid lonely darkness,
crying aloud in silence for happiness....
do you hear me?

When I first allowed you to enter my empty space,
I opened my heart to possible heartbreak....
now the tears won't stop!

When I....my love!

DEVIL'S AT MY DOORSTEP

{ { { screeching } } }
a scratch running down
the door, or my spine, like sharp
fingernails clawing
a barren chalkboard.

{ { { scraping } } }
up against my fear,
fear like moldy Romano
being brushed against
rough, abrasive skin.

{ { { slithering } } }
deep inside my mind,
all thoughts of happiness gone,
gone to the graveyard
of dismembered dreams.

A SEA OF EMOTION

{ { { seeping } } }
down into my ears,
the wheeze of malevolent
breath rotting,
rotting thoughts of you.

{ { { screaming } } }
as love disappears,
darkness and misery left.
I face my devils,
devils at my doorstep.

FORGOTTEN

"Heart in a Bottle #1"

Candlelight flickered madly,
leaping from the sting
of your words,
shadow dancing around
a partially devoured T-bone,
it's raw, pink center swimming
in a stagnant river of
A-1 sauce and blood-red juice,
like how my heart felt…

{ { { COLD } } }

You stole my love
and flipped it inside out.
How
could you not love me after all
we've been through?
Pictures on the walls encircled my eyes,
reeling, dizzy,
room spinning out of control.
Feeling sick, I began to sip
my ice water and~~~

A SEA OF EMOTION

floating, aimlessly adrift,
my heart imprisoned
inside an empty bottle of
Paul Masson, our love now done
before it's time.
I see you walking down the beach,
a rippling, dirty brown ribbon of sand,
receding, growing dimmer.

You turn and smile,
wave good-bye,

a shallow gleam in your eye.
Suddenly a wave shoves
me under, propelling me deeper towards
a cave of misbegotten tears.

Reaching, sinking, drowning,
gasping for air.

Breathe damn it, breathe.
I can't. I won't.
Without you I am nothing for
you've stolen

ALL I ever was.
Finally,
I break the surface,
water smoother now, like
a two-way mirror, your face
smiling back, but
I know you don't see me.

A seagull does though, dives
down and wildly pecks away
at my cell of glass,
hungry
for the decaying carrion within.
It screeches in anger…

flying off with nothing.
How you haunt my
every thought
with your indifference.
Harsh sun burning as I sail
to who knows where,
damned if l care.

Doomed
Just one more sad message,
lost

in another empty bottle.

DREAM OF ROSES

"Heart in a Bottle #2"

Still lost in melancholy,
I continue to float
upon my dream of roses, adrift
in your smiles beneath a plaintive sun,
at sea in your heedless words
of forgetfulness,
up and down
in sensual reticence,

~~~ undulating~~~

as you once let your fingers
roam in search of nectar,
honey bees crying out
with forgiveness.
My heart yet captured within
this bottle now polished'
in loneliness,

shackled…

in a silent prison
made of burning glass.
Bitter reflections of a love
tossed upon currents
that have no purpose, no
direction, devoid of feelings,

numb…

as another wave carries me
down a tunnel of screaming trains,
surrounded by the glare of
ebony fish-eyes,
mocking me with their
hungry desire to dine upon my
barely beating heart,

fish bait…

I crack the mirrored surface and
see an empty beach, glittering,
sun-encrusted. No~~
not barren after all, is that you?
My heart races towards shore on frothy whitecaps of
urgency

searching....

CAN LOVE BE TRUSTED?

"Heart in a Bottle #3"

The early, waxing moon rocked
to and fro in its cradle,
resplendent in robes
of orange and yellow sunflowers.
My bottle of spurned desires
floated ashore, washed by silky suds
of innocence, scrubbed
by absolving sand…purged.

A drunken horseshoe crab
staggers and strikes a wayward
claw against my conclave,
rousing me from months
of depressed meditation,
searching for elusive answers
within dark dissolution,
my magic mantra
reverberating, echoing…

{ { { I so want you back
want you back
want you
back } } }

KERRY MARZOCK

I can sense your nearness
on the breath of evening songs,
your name whispered by
fading starfish and
dried-up sand dollars.
My heart begins to race
a little faster as I
feel your hands pick me up,
caress my neck, and
pull out the cork
with quivering sighs.
My brooding disquietude
released on a mist of
desire, your eyes
the color of a balmy sunset.

My heart sings a song of gratitude
yet worry intercedes.
Your arms feel so good, but
can I trust you?

ON THE FAR SIDE OF TRANQUILITY

"Lift off, we have lift off at thirty-two
minutes past the hour. Lift off on
Apollo 11".
* * * * * *
I stare a hole
through time and space,
barely scratching the surface
to my resistance.
Mission Control has reported,
to my extreme distress,
a malfunction has occurred.
Love may be in trouble.
Is that really Neil's dark eyes
looking down upon me?
* * * * * *
"Houston, Tranquility Base here,
the Eagle has landed."

KERRY MARZOCK

* * * * * *

Closing my eyes 1 hear
the Sea of Fertility laughing,
mocking me,
a haunting voice
crooning "Blue Moon".
Your orbit locked,
making a landing of near
perfection upon my life in such
a tranquil docking of two
lonely hearts.
* * * * * *
"That's one small step for man,
one giant leap for mankind."
* * * * * *
I felt your touch
caress my anxious dreams as 1
took a nervous
step towards sweet desire,
then an excited leap as Apollo fired
it's after burners
and latched thankfully
upon my lunar module's surface,
swimming frantically in the
Sea of Tranquility.

A SEA OF EMOTION

* * * * * *

"Magnificent sight out here,
magnificent desolation."
* * * * * *
Lunar dust forever
reminding me that you stood here,
your footprints
to be a part of my dreams
for unending years, craters littered
with broken promises.
Ah~ Houston, we have splashdown!
Slowly sinking into empty waters
upon the far side of
tranquility.
* * * * * *

"Houston, do you copy?
We have a problem!"
* * * * * *

SANDS OF INNOCENCE

I stand proud
against this raging storm,
buffeted by these howling winds
that strike my skin with stinging sand

sands of accusation.
Should I carry this guilt for
desiring happiness over sadness?
I gaze at my footsteps being washed away

away from forgiveness
though I've given all I have.
My eyes cast their weariness upon
the eroded beach to lie beside dying tests

tests of sand dollars,
their spiny limbs praying
in remorse, the center star leading
me afar as the shepherds went in search

A SEA OF EMOTION

searching for truth
and understanding, hearing
the singing sand of Death Valley
booming like thunder across my memory

memories of a life
so fraught with deep rivers
and wide valleys, knowing my time has
finally come to lie on these sands of innocence.

TREE OF LONELINESS

Barren ~~ isolated ~~ alone,
steely gray clouds in dismal skies
spreading my whispers upon lonely sighs.

This grizzled tree now with heart of stone,
leafless ~ devoid of life ~ tears drip from forlorn eyes,
naked branches beseeching as all hope dies.

Your love the sweetest I've ever known.
Those expressive eyes ~ that smile ~ a dream I realize
I dare not lose ~ a love I need to memorize.

Gray skin ~ bark dried and cracked ~ not my own.
Gazing up at a shadowed moon through vacant cries,
wondering if I will ever see you smile again at sunrise.

Small branches ~ thin and fragile—silently windblown,
empty fingers reaching for one more day in paradise,
atop a frigid pond barely dressed in gossamer ice.

Frozen ground around my feet now moss-grown, roots forever
lost~ disoriented ~ heartbeat slowly dies, praying you can hear
my tearful goodbyes.

BITER WORDS

Your bitter words of acrimony
lay sadly upon me like a combination
of icy fingers and frigid thoughts that freeze
my tears upon my face inside the hot culmination
of sorrow and heartache that is now our destiny
under a sun that has lost its once brilliant
afterglow, our love no longer resilient
inside this aftermath of despair,
so lost within a nightmare,
now painfully aware
you just don't care,
as my eyes stare
into thin air,
nowhere,
no fair!
I care!
Good-
bye!
I~~
cry!
*
*
*

THE LADY FROM YESTERDAY

Soft, feathery dreams,
she moves with such fluid grace,
gray, nighttime shadows.
*

Her lips sweet roses,
red wine on a summer day.
Blood paints stars' silver.
* *

Her smile bright sunshine,
echoes of warm caresses
fading to darkness.
* * *

Her touch electric,
sultry breeze so sensual,
difficult to breathe.

A SEA OF EMOTION

* * * *

Her fingers on fire,
icy folds of deep desire.
Ashes left burning.
* * * *

Her eyes like black pearls.
Never ending galaxy,
a dead sea now screams.
* * * * * *

To forever be
the Lady from Yesterday,
thief of lonely dreams!
* * * * * * *

WHEN BLACKBIRDS FLY

I stand alone,
a silent shadow!
My mind fears
a solitary sky
of somber blackbirds.
Two feisty chipmunks,
tails held high
like tiny spears
mock my sorrow
with salty words.
Blue magpies chatter
their wary warning,
"Please be careful."
Over and over!
A smiling stone
quietly whispers hello.
Wiping away tears
as roses sigh,
heart now hollow,
your name windblown
on feelings shattered.
Sad eyes mourning
when blackbirds fly!

THE LONELY SHROUD

A thick, dirty gray pallor of sorrow's song
slides eerily over an early morning of lost dreams.
Harsh rain falls ominously, mimicking the forlorn,
drumming cadence of tomorrow's wistful heart,
for l dreamt of you once more.
All night long!

Naked, spiteful trees stand at crooked attention,
spreading their beckoning, pleading arms
in beseeching supplication.
They hauntingly pray for me,
like lonely, sobbing gendarmes
who know my dreams still go unanswered.

A lonely crow stares my way from across the road,
beady eyes narrow and pensive, as if it knows
all my deepest secrets and inner desires.
Desires submerged in sobbing rainbows.
Once bright colors now lost in destiny's fires.

My disappearing dream still calling your name,
I silently shut a somber front door,
pull the blinds, and turn out harsh lights
that bathe my confused thoughts of nevermore.
Darkness draws me back to reclaim
the soft embrace of midnight.

IN THE DARKNESS

They mostly come within the night.
Mostly!

In the dark, like some malingering,
malicious creatures that have
never felt the light before.

They've come to steal your dreams
away with murderous intent,
snickering, slithering, smothering
you with their evil screams.

Your heart pounding, barely beating,
afraid their hounds of hell
might smell your fear,
hear the sound
of shallow, broken breathing.

Scared the nightmares might pervade
your mind where happy dreams might dwell.
It's so damn dark in here.
Can you hear the screaming jangle of chains
being drug across the floor to be wrapped
around your fear, and emphasize the pain?

Sheer evil from some primeval scream,
oh God, where is the hope?
The light of day, the way to dream,
they're coming, I can smell
the burning stench of hell.
I feel their claws! They sense my fright.
Thank God, the light.

PANIC

The glittering sun, once aglow with promise and hope,
is suddenly blanketed with a shroud of bitter darkness.
A menacing cloud so thick with ominous intent
that it splinters your laughter,
making it nearly impossible to think, smile,
or even cope with this ordinary life.
Once strong willpower dissolving as if it never existed,
strength now supplanted with total weakness.

Every nerve ending still alive, screaming loudly,
"Help Me! Oh God, please help me!"
to anyone brave enough to listen.
But they don't hear your cries.
You are alone!

Evil fingertips of ripping barbed wire crawling like red-hot
pokers through every screaming vein
like malicious, electric eels.
Tortured body now covered with sinister bugs,
slowly creeping and scratching against
every square inch of exposed skin,
all senses now completely awakened and raw.
PANIC seizing your crippled mind with a steel paw
surrounded by a strangling, maniacal grin.
Once a world of promise, now lathered
with searing, white-hot pain.

A SEA OF EMOTION

A mocking, evil voice screaming in your ear,
"You can't do anything!"
Once strong and brave, now reduced to rubble,
cowering within never-ending fear.
But still nobody hears your plea.
You are alone!

Out of control heartbeats slamming frantically
inside your chest against shattered walls.
Pounding in sheer terror while being swept
down a river of deriding laughter.
Kidnapped from happiness and now propelled
towards a cliff of impending doom.
Boiling blood rushing like undulating, viscous oil
towards a disastrous waterfall of emotions.
Blue sky now reluctantly replaced with darkened,

unfulfilled dreams from a lost and fractured moon.
Once brave, I cower behind my crumbling balustrade.
Riddled body now hollow from the impact
of so many murderous arrows coated
with poisonous words of,
"I am so damn afraid!"
Screams of pain still going unanswered,
locked in a solitary prison of hopeless misery.
You remain painfully alone.

With sizzling tears pouring forth
from a bottomless vacuum of hopeless dreams,
you continue to reach out.
Fingertips blood-stained from
scratching and clawing to save what's left of sanity.

As hopeless as it seems, you still try to survive.

Suddenly through this sickening curtain of
evil thoughts appear the palm of a hand,
reaching for you,
pleading for you to grab a hold.
You shudder with relief,
realizing somebody did hear your distress calls.

Far from saved,
you force the barest of smiles
as Death and its disciples slither away.
screaming their loss of your soul.
Thankfully a shallow light appears in the darkness.
It's the light of at least one more day.

CREATURE #1

"Fears"
Through dark, smothering shadows of teardrops
crouch those blazing, red-hot eyes.
They painfully pierce my desires like hungry fires,
hiding their monstrous intentions
until the welcoming arms of moonrise.

I shiver fearfully as claws of the creature sweep
all my sturdy walls of bravery away.
From a frightful mouth of lost dreams seep
frozen screams that chill my forlorn thoughts
like melting ice cubes on a hot, summer day.

Those demonic eyes seem to furtively creep forward
on stalking paws like thirsty red fingertips
bathed inside moonlight from blood of the ox.
I turn and run, moving quickly away
from this blackened window to my soul.
Behind crimson teardrops I realize that all time
has come to a silent stop from shattered clocks.

Within the bedroom I slink back from a quivering door.
Across the mirror I see my name written in tears,
harshly emblazoned on a blood-red tombstone.
In the shimmering glass the creature stares back at me.
I cry out in painful agony as I realize that those
pleading eyes are but my own fears.
The creature is me!

CREATURE #2

"Lost Love"
Like a mysterious, grinning black cat that slinks
through your hopes and dreams,
this creature of broken hearts screams in hellish
glee at malicious thoughts of stealing away
all feelings of love you once tastefully relished.
Inside painful tears, I sob uncontrollably as love
sadly, shrinks through a darkened doorway.

With an angry sweep of a sinful claw
it swipes away the silkiness of your loving touch.
It erases the smooth, velvety glow of your
lips I once smoothly brushed with mine so much.
Those glittering blue pools of your eyes I used
to dreamily look into and forever fall ~~
now empty, with a mere twitch of its hateful tail.

A SEA OF EMOTION

With blood-covered fangs it eats away
at my urges and needs like hungry termites
tearing down the wailing wall of our love.
This creature devours all dreams of wistful nights
inside blazing flames of hells fire.
Darkened clouds of loss drape over me from above.
Sweet visions of you disappearing with wounded desires.

As it creeps slowly into the frigid throes of midnight
those devouring eyes of this love thief peer back
at me with a laughing, spiteful sneer.
My loneliness now echoing off blank walls
of a cracked and broken heart.
Wondering if I will ever again embrace love's delight
as this creature leaves only my disheartened tears.

CREATURE#3

"Stolen Dreams"
Hissing like an angry steam engine
I can hear the insipid voice of horror.
The frightening creature has appeared once more,
to steal away all hope, invade my dreams,
and painfully snatch your love beyond my screams.

It slithers against my staggering mind,
causing distant visions of your face to blur.
Like shimmering heat waves from a far off oasis,
I reach into the rippling air before me.
Your smile and voice fade within my own Dead Sea.

Terrifying jaws of the beast widen slowly,
fangs sinking like daggers into desperate dreams.
Dreams of your love and our life together,
sins of the serpent drip words unholy,
as thoughts of you are stolen from my heart forever.

I feel the poison from this creature crawl
though my veins and sour the taste of your sweet lips,
steal away the glitter of your eyes as it screams
apart your embrace from my reaching fingertips.

All final thoughts of you now stolen away
upon fragments of shattered moonbeams.
Now standing atop a bleak highway,
I'm forever lost without my dreams.

BLOOD ON THE MOON

Staring at a heartless moon through waves of fear,
you feel not my pain, nor hear these tears.
My world now fractured by a hammer of despair,
true thoughts of love no longer there.

I cry under a desperate moon not made of Swiss cheese.
More like dark craters from shattered pieces
of my numb and ruptured heart. Life now split apart
to forever battle the pain that broken love releases.

I feel your silent gaze brush the stillness of my face.
That loving, gentle caress I once embraced.
Those magical fingers, like fragments of moon dust,
now tearfully fading away without a trace.

Reaching down, I grasp a quivering red rose that bites.
An angry thorn screams out, "Good-bye!"
In my mind I hear a scarlet teardrop cry out your name,
while lost love sobs amid crimson moonlight.

I lift the rose above my head towards darkened skies,
stars now painted with deceitful lies.
Thorn now crying, petals dying, our love forever lost.
My blood upon the moon now sighs.

KERRY MARZOCK

A LONELY POET

I am just a lonely poet
lost in a drawer of misplaced words.
A life fragmented with broken promises and
shattered dreams now softly sung by
lonesome, somber blackbirds.

Standing alone once again on a barren shore
I cast out my life into a troubled sea
of ragged, painful memories,
hoping to discover at last that true love is not
just one more tearfully painted metaphor.

Echoes bouncing from forlorn keys,
tumbling and stumbling blindly into each other
on a stark sheet of solitary whiteness.
There is no feeling, no emotion, forever sightless,
whispered sadly in a chorus of silent pleas.

I reach for you with outstretched hand,
fingerprints forever burned from love and sorrow.
Tears have stained and blurred the dreams
we fondly held of just one more happy tomorrow,
my beach now lonely, devoid of sand.

I'm now so lost atop a sea of lonely letters,
floating aimlessly on waves of despair,
awash with tears sobbing nevermore.
For I am just a lonely poet
watching love die inside this silent prayer.

A SEA OF EMOTION

YOU TAKE MY BREATH AWAY~ ~

~ ~ ~ like the velvet whisper of morning dew,
sweet desire for you endlessly entrapped.
How my urgent body tingles.
This inflamed heart of mine
now all but awaits
to feel your lavish touch,
your warm and rich embrace,
the fire and passion I can always find
when safely held with the arms of only you.
* * * * * *

Some parts of love just are ~
While some have sadly passed ~
Some love eagerly rests upon a star ~
While sometimes romance will forever last ~
* * * * * *

How I can feel your breath
skim so softly against my skin,
like a kiss from lips of pure damask.
Your soft fingertips like blades of grass
that can so arouse deep passions,
that forever stoke this fire
of my complete desire
for simply
you.

KERRY MARZOCK

BRIDGE OF DISCOVERY

Standing at one end of the bridge
I stared into thick, swirling mist that
wickedly whispered to me ~~
"Come see for yourself, if you dare."
The voice was low, sensual,
like a warm embrace
that sliced through midnight air
with the seeming intent
to erase my last
remnants of indecision.
I slowly started forward,
legs and feet imprisoned in my fear,
not wishing to know
the truth, but....
needing to see and hear
who I truly was.
Confusion reigned ~
anger stained ~
desire uncontained ~
I stood atop that bridge of sighs
and peered into my future.
Fog curled poetically before peering eyes.
Then a movement, a shadow,
the apparition of an angel appearing
through the shroud.
Beautiful ~ enchanting ~ alluring ~
she reached for me.

Smiling, I blended
into her arms.
The mist cleared and I walked away.
Unconfused, no longer lonely,
I had finally reached inside the mirror
on my bridge of discovery,
relieved there would at least
be one more tomorrow.

WHAT IF TODAY....

What if today....
was the day....
my dreams came true?
What if all eroded yesterdays
became my hopes of warm tomorrows?
What if today...
was the day...
I said good-bye to you?
What if I slowly walked away
through tears of misbegotten sorrows?
What if...
What's the use, for
what ifs are only lost desires
of dreams and promises unfulfilled.
Embers ablaze from bonfires
of guilty heroes.
Then I smile and wonder....
but what if today....
was the day....

A Sea of Emotion is simply a book of everyday life. Everyone who dreams of that never-ending love or special friendship will find meaning within the pages of this unique book of poetry. As we struggle through life, heading for our final destination, we find many adventures and heartbreaks along the way—loves we wish we could reclaim, enjoyable events we wish we could relive, and of course, family that is so dear to our hearts.

We stop along our lifelong journey to find injustices, greed, dishonesty, suffering, and all the wrongs of mankind in our modern world. Yet we also find love, honesty, sharing, and caring on a never-ending *Sea of Emotion*. Come along on life's little journey as you turn every page and realize that others believe in the same way of life as you. Through these pages you'll find sadness, love, family ties, and loneliness all adrift on *A Sea of Emotion*.

Born in Greensburg, Pennsylvania, in 1947, I was gifted with an instinct for sports, a love of animals, and a passion for the written word. To become a published writer has been a lifelong dream. A lifetime of searching and discovery has provided me with a wealth of experiences, not all easily handed to me or earned. I moved from Lancaster, Pennsylvania, to Philadelphia where I have lived for the past thirty years with Richard and with Rain the wonder dog for the past three years.